Tom Grainger,
#305 - 1950 Robson Street,
Vancouver, B.C.
V6G 1E8

Inquiries from outside Canada regarding rights to produce The Injured should be directed to:

Hope Leresche & Steele,
Drama Department,
11 Jubilee Place,
Chelsea, London SW3 3TE,
England.

Additional copies of this play may be obtained for $3.00 each plus 25¢ postage per copy from:

Playwrights Co-op,
344 Dupont Street,
Toronto, Ontario.
M5R 1V9

A catalogue and supplements listing over 200 published Canadian plays, as well as lists of plays especially suitable for High Schools, Community Theatres and Children's Theatres, are available from the Playwrights Co-op, free of charge.

1st Edition, March, 1976

Grainger, Tom.
The injured

ISBN 0-919834-46-9 pa.

I. Title.

PS8513.R26I55 C812'.5'4 C76-017043-6
PR9199.3.G73I55

THE INJURED won the first annual Clifford E. Lee Award in 1974 and was first produced at the Studio Theatre, Edmonton, January 9th, 1975, with the following cast:

JUD SLATER......................Michael Forrest

SARAH SLATER......................Janet Daverne

MISS ROGERS..................Heather MacCallum

HARRY PLATT......................David Diamond

TESS SLATER......................Lilene Mansell

MATT SLATER........................Bill Meilen

YOUNG SARAH......................Crystal Fleuty

Scenic and costume designer John W. Graham

Director Howard Dallin

CHARACTERS: (in the order in which they speak)

SARAH SLATER	Early fifties. Wife of Jud.
JUD	Early fifties. Spinning room overlooker.
MISS ROGERS	Schoolteacher. Twenty-one.
HARRY PLATT	A tramp. Early thirties.
MATT SLATER	Father of Jud. Early forties.
TESS SLATER	Matt's wife. Late thirties.
YOUNG SARAH	At age fourteen.

SETTING:

The action of the play takes place in the graveyard of the industrial town of Loston in Lancashire and in an isloated cottage a mile or so from the town and near the canal which skirts the town.

Only a suggestion of a multiple setting is needed. Four vases in a row downstage centre represent the graveyard. One white vase has wings for handles. OUR is on one wing. NELLIE is on the other. There is a small generator downstage left of centre. An old bicycle leans against it. Near it two kitchen chairs. Up from these and to the left a double bed placed up and down. Chairs stand guard on each side of it. On a raised platform up from the double bed and to the left and placed across stage there is a narrow single bed, with a chair to the right of it. To the right of the single bed and almost centre stage there is a lectern with a big scrapbook on it. The book is closed. The cover of it is a gaudy red. OUR BABY is writ large on it in silver. To the right of the lectern and downstage of it there is a round table with four chairs. Flats in patterns of black and white close off the upstage area except for a door on the right. Lighting will turn sections of these patterns into portraits during the course of the play. The portraits are of "Our Nellie", a beautiful, happy girl in her very early teens, and of Harry Platt, a tramp aged about thirty. He has a boyish, laughing face, and wears a cloth cap set at a rakish angle. "Our Nellie" does not appear in the play. Black flats close off the sides except for a door down right.

We need only the bare bones of the setting. The generator is in a shed outside the cottage, but as we do not need the cottage neither do we need the shed. Although not shown in the setting there is a back door to the cottage near the shed which houses the generator. The characters would normally enter through down right door when they have been outside other than to the "shed", when the back door would be used. The actors must move through the setting as though through rooms. Care must be taken to make these movements real. What has happened was real. What is happening is real. What will happen must seem inevitable.

A scrim separates the four vases from the rest of the setting.

NOTE: Scenes 4 and 8 are continuations of Scene 1 and must be so played.

THE INJURED

ACT I

Scene 1: The Graveyard

SARAH stands to the right of the vases facing left. She is dressed entirely in black. Solid and implacable she stands above JUD, who kneels up from the vases in his good blue serge suit and shiny boots, with a new cloth cap set dead centre on his big grey head.

SARAH's voice is clear and strong. She speaks not only to JUD, but to the bones in the rotting boxes beneath the sod and clay. She has said these words before, many times. She will speak them again, many times.

SARAH: Pray, our Jud.

JUD: (Raises his head, lets arms hang limp)
Gentle Jesus, meek and mild,
Look upon this little child.

SARAH: A child, Jud Slater. Suffer to come unto Me, little children. Suffer, Jud. (Abruptly) Whose child then?

JUD: Mine, Sarah. Mine and thine.

SARAH: I bore her. When I was but fourteen I bore her. I gave her suck. Her were all lovely. Her were that nice I used to kiss her all over every time I changed her. I bore that child with every hand and tongue against me.

JUD: Not mine, Sarah. Not mine.

SARAH: Especially thine, Jud. You hoped we'd both go under. Be honest. Didn't you hope we'd both go under, then you'd be shut of us?

JUD: I'm bound to admit that I did. I were too young to be trapped like that. Then I saw the babby. Her were a bonny babby.

SARAH: Pray.

JUD: Oh Jesus take care of our Nellie. Heal her torn and broken body Jesus. Make --- Oh Christ what a bloody farce.

SARAH: Go on.

JUD: Make her all lovely again and keep her for us till we come. Oh my holy roasting suffering crucified Jesus bloody Christ. There's naught below this sod but bones, Sarah. There's naught above but sun and moon and stars and weather. It's... it's daft.

SARAH: What are you, Jud Slater?

JUD: A beast, Sarah. A beast of the fields.

SARAH: What else?

JUD: It were an accident. I tell thee it were an accident.

SARAH: What are you, Jud Slater? What else?

JUD: (A sudden screamshout as he rears back, then falls sobbing on the grave)
FORGIVE ME!

(Blackout)

Scene Two: The Lodger

The vases have disappeared. The scrim rises. SARAH and JUD sit at the round table with its Sundays only fancy white cloth on it. SARAH wears her black dress. JUD has taken off his tie and jacket. They are draped over one of the chairs near the double bed. SARAH's coat is draped over the other. If the table could groan it would do so from the weight of the near indigestibles on it. There is wicked looking tea in the big blue and white teapot. No teacups here, but solid mugs that hold a good half pint. Strong Lancashire pawnshop stomachs, take anything in, wait to counter yet another attack.

SARAH puts a piece of pie on a plate and passes it to JUD. She then pours his tea before helping herself.

SARAH: Flossie all right?

JUD: She'll do.

SARAH: Funny nobody came.

JUD: There's time yet.
(Silence but for the chomping of teeth, the sound of knives and forks on china)
They all want to live in town. Where there's lights and noise. They can't stand the dark. Can't stand quiet.

SARAH: There's no room in town.

JUD: Them Pakis. Sleep twenty to a room. On the floor.
(Silence but for the chomping of teeth, the long swallows of tea)

SARAH: There'll be enough potato pie left for you to take to work tomorrow.

JUD: I'm sick of bloody work. Don't remind me of it.

SARAH: I made it big enough for three. I could have sworn we'd have got somebody today. You can get one of your Pakis to warm it up for you.

JUD: I'll eat it cold. You should just see what they put in that oven. You should just see the muck they eat.
(Silence again)

SARAH: Funny nobody came.

JUD: We can manage without lodgers.

SARAH: (With a little truculence) What about the future then? Happen old Horrocks'll lay his hand on your shoulder one day soon.

JUD: (Flatly) Old Horrocks has never laid his hand on my shoulder in his life.

SARAH: All the more reason for bewaring him when he does then. He'll lay his hand on your shoulder that day, our Jud.

JUD: What day? What if he does? What day are you on about?

SARAH: The day he says we won't need you next week, Jud. The day he says go down and get your cards.

JUD: (Slams mug down on table) Why should he say that?
(Rises and stands over her. Speaks slowly, as though to a backward child)
I've worked for him upwards of thirty year.
(Moves away, stands near the lectern. His hand traces OUR BABY on it)
Pour me some tea.

SARAH: (As though he has not moved, speaks to the chair where he had been sitting)
It's happened to better men than you, Jud. Look at all them colliers. Throwing their money away with both hands year after year. Clubs. Betting shops. The telly. Cocktail cabinets. Gramophones. Motor cars. Then one day a piece of paper in the wage packet.

JUD: (Turns to her) They got redundancy pay.

SARAH: And they spent it. Where's their redundancy pay today?

JUD: (Approaches, stands over her) What's all this to do with me? I told you to pour me some tea.

SARAH: (Pours tea as she talks at the chair)
It's got this to do with you. We don't buy things with our money. Straight in the bank. Every Monday morn, rain or shine, the happy walk to the bank for your Sarah. And not the savings bank either. The Midland. Safe. I do it for you, Jud. When the day comes them Pakis make old Horrocks sack you you can tell him to put the job where the monkey put the nuts. They'll demand one of their own as overlooker soon, you see if they don't.

JUD: One of their own.
(Picks up mug and drinks)
Put some more sugar in that. Three of 'em together couldn't do it. Ali can't even splice a belt. What's the country coming to when you've got an assistant overlooker who can't splice a belt? You can't tell 'em anything. They won't listen. They use their earholes for arseholes, most of 'em.

SARAH: (As though there has been no interruption)
When that day comes you can tell old Horrocks that your Sarah will see you don't starve. Your Sarah will see you have a home.

JUD: (Moves away. Shivers) This is a cold room.

SARAH: It's a cold house.

JUD: Yon kitchen's warm. We should eat in the kitchen.

SARAH: (Complacently) We always eat our tea in here, Jud.

JUD: (Braces himself, approaches, stands over her)
This is my house.

SARAH: (Rises, faces him. There is a change in the relationship. Each knows what the other is going to say)
Ours, Jud. Ours.

JUD: It was my dad's. Now it's mine.

SARAH: Your dad's been gone a long time, Jud.

JUD: (Retreats left) Ay.

SARAH: (Follows him) You know what he died of, don't you, Jud?

JUD: (Retreats further) Ay.

SARAH: (Follows him) Say it then. Say what he died of.

JUD: (Stands still, blank eyes avoiding her)
Shame, Sarah. My dad died of shame.

SARAH: (Sharply) What did my mam die of then?

JUD: Grief. Grief killed your mother, Sarah.

SARAH: Who caused it then? Say who caused it.

JUD: (Hopelessly) Let me be. It's work tomorrow. Let me be.

SARAH: (Relents) Who do you love then?
(Silence)
Say who you love then.
(Silence)
Say who you love.

JUD: (Turns head further away from her)
You, Sarah. Only you.

SARAH: Go on.

JUD: (By rote) You're that bonny, our Sarah.
(Slowly moves backward left away from her)
I mun have you.
(Turns suddenly and escapes quickly, slows down and stops left of the double bed)

SARAH: Where are you off to?
(Moves back to the table, sits)
What did I pour this tea for then?
(JUD stand motionless for a moment, then his hand goes to his mouth. He feels at his top teeth. His fingers go in and around as though adjusting a denture plate. His other hand goes to his mouth. He pushes up on his teeth)

JUD: Bugger these teeth.
(Stands motionless with his hands to his mouth, then lowers his hands and stands as though peering through a window. He calls without turning away)
Sarah!
(After a moment)
Sarah, come here!

SARAH: (Still sitting at table, shouts) What is it then?

JUD: (Without moving) I said come in here.

SARAH: (Rises) All right then.
(Crosses and stands right of the double bed)
What is it then?

JUD: (Does not look at her, nods his head)
Do you think yon might be your new lodger?

SARAH: (Moves quickly, stands near JUD, peers through "window". Her face relaxes. She almost smiles)
She might.

JUD: Her's a young un.

SARAH: That'll do. Young or not you'll leave her alone.

JUD: It'll be too quiet for her here. I'd be inclined to tell her it's been taken. That's a fair bike she's got. It's as near as dammit brand new.

SARAH: That room's been empty long enough. If she wants it she can have it. One week's rent in advance. Every Saturday. One week in advance.

JUD: Don't tell me. Tell her.

(MISS ROGERS enters extreme downstage left wheeling her bicycle. She leans it against the edge of the flat and stands for a moment looking around. She then crosses the stage and goes up to the door down right, looking around and up as she does so as though looking at a house or trying to catch sight of the people in it.

CONT'D She hesitates a moment and gazes up and around again before knocking on the door. She is twenty-one and lovely, auburn haired and fine skinned, with eyes like bobby dazzlers, big and greeny. Her long hair is tied by a ribbon at the back. Her hair shines. Her skin has a sheen on it. Her teeth are white and nearly perfect. The benefits of the "Welfare State", filched from the poor, have been lavished on her. She is from that other England. The England that is not "north". She possesses a small facile talent for drawing and daubing and a certificate from a Teacher's Training College which proves her to be a step or two ahead of slum children unless, hardly likely, one of them has a touch of genius. The dialogue between SARAH and JUD is not interrupted as she crosses the stage)

SARAH: She's not a mill lass.

JUD: That she's not. She's a bonny lass.

SARAH: You keep your eyes down and your mouth shut when she comes in, do you hear?

JUD: Ay.

SARAH: (As she moves away) Front door, Jud. Bring her into the parlour.
(Crosses and sits at table. JUD moves away from the bed. He goes as though through rooms to the door down right. He gets there as MISS ROGERS knocks again)

JUD: (A hand goes to his teeth as he nears the door) My gums are as nesh as a baby's.

MISS ROGERS: (As JUD opens door) Good afternoon. I am at the right place? You are Mr. Slater?

JUD: (Unmoving and unblinking) Ay.

MISS ROGERS: You advertised for a lodger. The card outside the newsagent's shop. Is the room still vacant?

JUD: Ay. (Moves aside) Come in.
(MISS ROGERS enters, advances a step or two and waits as JUD closes the door. After he has closed it he turns slowly and stands with his back to it. His unblinking gaze does not leave MISS ROGERS' face)

MISS ROGERS: (After a moment, with a smile) May I see the room?

JUD: It's quiet here. Too quiet for some folks.

MISS ROGERS: I like quiet... My name is Rogers. Pamela Rogers.

JUD: (Unblinking gaze still on her face)
Ay. Well, you know my name.

MISS ROGERS: May I see the room?

JUD: You'll have to see Sarah first.
(Goes slowly up to her)
She's in the parlour.
(Keeps on moving)
It's this way. Sarah's in charge of all arrangements. I've nowt to do with it.
(MISS ROGERS follows him as he goes as though along a passageway and through a door to SARAH at the table)
This is Miss Rogers, Sarah, about the room.

SARAH: I know it's about the room, Jud. What else could it be about? Sit down, miss.
(MISS ROGERS sits)
The last girl we had worked at the carpet factory... We don't need you, Jud.

JUD: Ay... Well, I'll happen see you later, lass.
(MISS ROGERS looks up and smiles briefly at him. He goes slowly left and down)

SARAH: She didn't last long. Said it was too quiet for her. You're not at the carpet factory then?

MISS ROGERS: Carpet factory? No, I'm a schoolteacher. I'll be at the new secondary modern school.
(JUD is near the generator. He reaches behind it and brings out a bit of clean white rag. He sits and wipes the generator housing. The wipe is the next thing to a caress)

SARAH: I don't want to keep chopping and changing. I want somebody to take that room and stay for a decent while.

MISS ROGERS: If I like the room I'll be here for quite some time.

SARAH: The rent must be paid weekly in advance. Six pounds a week. For that you get your bed, your breakfast and your tea every day. Washing's extra if you want me to do it.

MISS ROGERS: I don't think that would be necessary.

SARAH: (Rises) I'll take you to see the room then.

MISS ROGERS: Yes, it's no good discussing terms till I've seen the room.

SARAH: (Moving as though through rooms approaches the single bed. MISS ROGERS follows a step or two behind)
There'll be no discussion of terms. Six pounds is what I want and six pounds is what I'll get.
(SARAH stands to the right of the bed. MISS ROGERS moves around, then stands as though looking at a view through a window. JUD stops wiping the generator, puts his feet up on the other chair and lights a cigarette)

JUD: Work tomorrow, Flossie... I can't stand the heat in yon spinning room as well as I did... Still, it's somewhere to go. Gets me away from her. Heat doesn't mean a thing to them Pakis. It's always hot in Pakiland. They don't even work up a sweat. If they went any slower rigor bloody mortis would set in.

SARAH: It's not fancy, but it is clean.

MISS ROGERS: It will do, Mrs. Slater. All I want is a place to sleep and keep my clothes and read.

SARAH: You read then, do you?

JUD: The old-time spinners used to work up a rare old sweat. When they died they went down there to cool off. Surprising how many were religious, though. Chapel mainly. Methodist. Blue serge suits and stiff white collars every mortal Sunday. No pubs for them. Temperance bars. Temperance bloody bars. All singing "Jerusalem". England's green and pleasant land my arse.

SARAH: You'll take it then?

MISS ROGERS: Yes. I don't suppose I would find anything else in a hurry.

SARAH: That you wouldn't. There's folk gone grey hereabouts looking for somewhere to live.

JUD: (Takes feet off chair and wipes the seat with the bit of rag)
It's a long time since anybody sat in that. Harry used to sit in it, but that were years since. Years and years.

SARAH: We'll go back to the parlour then. You can settle up in there.
(SARAH and MISS ROGERS go back to the table and sit)

JUD: (Gently wipes the generator housing)
Yon's a bonny lass. That skin. There's real peaches and cream for you... Them eyes.

SARAY: That'll be six pounds then, miss.

MISS ROGERS: (Opens her purse and counts out the money)
There you are, Mrs. Slater. I'll move in right away.

SARAH: Will you need a rent book?

MISS ROGERS: It's not necessary. I would like a receipt, though.

SARAH: I'll give you one later.
(Picks up the money)
You won't regret it. You'll soon settle in. We eat well here. What food costs today.

MISS ROGERS: My things are at the station. Could you arrange to have them picked up?

SARAH: No sooner said than done, miss.
(Calls, more a scream than a shout)
Jud!

JUD: She'll scream her head off one day, Floss. It'll go screaming through the clouds to Liverpool. To Ireland. They'll call it a banshee there. We'll be left with a body without its head.

SARAH: What do you teach then?

MISS ROGERS: Art. I may have to teach something else as well.

SARAH: I should think you'll have to. There's not much room for art in Loston.

JUD: I'll plant it here in the back. Or tie an old flywheel to it and drop it in the cut.

SARAH: Where are you, our Jud?

JUD: All right then.
(Leaves the rag on the generator housing)
See you later, Floss. Be good.
(Moves away right, then turns and goes far left to MISS ROGER's bicycle, examines it)

SARAH: You might as well have your tea. I'll bet you're starved. How far have you come?

MISS ROGERS: From Wimborne.

SARAH: (Without comprehension) Oh yes... I'll get you a cup.
(Rises and goes off through upstage door)

JUD: It's a fair bike, all right.
(His hand touches and caresses the seat)
That lovely backside's been on here.
(His hand goes to his mouth, presses up against his top teeth. He turns, makes his way quickly to the table as SARAH enters upstage carrying a mug and cutlery)

SARAH: There you are then.
(Sits at table, pours tea. JUD stands left of table)
We like our tea strong. I hope you do.
(Passes a mug to MISS ROGERS)
Help yourself to milk and sugar, miss... She's taken the room, Jud.

JUD: (Stares unblinkingly at SARAH)
Does she know we haven't got a telly then?

SARAH: She knows.

JUD: Does she know the lavatory's outside?

SARAH: She knows, Jud.

JUD: (Moves nearer to the table, eyes still on SARAH)
Does she know we haven't got a bathroom then?

SARAH: She knows. You're to bring her things from the station.
Give him the ticket, miss.

JUD: This room's cold. We only eat our tea in here.

SARAH: She knows that, Jud.

JUD: (Moves away, ends up near the lectern)
We have a hip bath. We use it in the kitchen. It's warm in there. You can use it whenever you like, miss. Twice a week if you like. I'll get it ready for you, then skedaddle. We have our bath Saturdays, but we wouldn't expect you to use the same water. That wouldn't be right.

SARAH: She'll have her baths at the school. She's at the new school. They have shower baths and all there. And the telly.
(Nods in a proprietary way at MISS ROGERS)
She teaches art.

JUD: Fancy that! It'll be a bit of a comedown for her living here, won't it?

SARAH: That's for her to judge and for you to keep quiet about. Get down to that station and get her things.

JUD: It's nowt much here, miss. But then, we don't expect much, do we, Sarah?

SARAH: Them as expect never receive.

MISS ROGERS: I'll manage nicely, Mr. Slater. I'll be able to take my easel into the fields. My art master used to say that if you can paint a cow you can paint anything.

JUD: You'll not go short of cows.
(Goes behind lectern)
Does she know there's only the one tap?

SARAH: She knows. She's paid her first week's rent. Cash on the nail.

JUD: (His hand traces OUR BABY on the front of the scrapbook)
Does she know about this then?

SARAH: (Contemptuously) How's Flossie then?

JUD: Does she know?

SARAH: Flossie's his friend, miss. (Jeeringly) Isn't Flossie your friend?

MISS ROGERS: His... his girl friend, Mrs. Slater?

SARAH: She's a powerful lass if she is. All the lights in this house come from her. Flossie's his generator. He spends most of his spare time with her. Don't you, Jud?

MISS ROGERS: His generator?

SARAH: Come from behind there, Jud. Get her things from the station.

JUD: (Moves away from the lectern)
She doesn't know then?

SARAH: She's not from these parts. She's from Wimborne, wherever that is.

MISS ROGERS: It's in Dorset. I think it's very self-reliant of you to make your own electricity, Mr. Slater. Very individualistic. I think it's super that a man should stand on his own two feet like that.

JUD: It weren't a question of standing on me own two feet, miss. It were a lot cheaper to buy a generator than to pay that lot to put the electric in. Bugger the Electricity Board.

SARAH: Language, Jud. His dad had the water laid on. What that must have cost. Off you go. Give him the ticket then.

MISS ROGERS: (Takes tickets from her purse)
There are two suitcases. Black leather ones. Are you sure you'll be able to manage them.

JUD: (Takes tickets) I'll tie them on to the bike. I'll manage.

SARAH: Take something to eat, miss. There's plenty left.

JUD: I'll be off then.

SARAH: (Without looking at him) That's right, Jud.
(JUD goes down to his bicycle, which leans against the generator. He picks up the rag and wipes the seat, then adjusts the front wheel)

MISS ROGERS: I am rather hungry. (Points at the pie) What's this?

SARAH: Potato pie. Try a bit.
(Puts a piece on a plate and passes it. MISS ROGERS' gingerly tests it with her fork)
Have you never had potato pie afore?

MISS ROGERS: No. Is it a northern dish?

SARAH: It's a poor folks dish. We used to live on it at one time.
(JUD wheels his bike left. He stops for a moment near MISS ROGERS' bicycle, briefly caresses the seat, then goes off)

MISS ROGERS: It's quite tasty, actually.

SARAH: You'll get used to it. Happen I should have warmed it up for you.

MISS ROGERS: It's quite all right.

SARAH: I'd better tell you about the rules.

MISS ROGERS: Rules?

SARAH: There's only two. No visitors, miss. No visitors at any time. We don't have visitors, so why should you?

MISS ROGERS: Why indeed? What's the other rule?

SARAH: We go to bed early. We want quiet after that. No traipsing about down here while we're in bed. Our bedtime is your bedtime. He works hard. He needs his sleep.

MISS ROGERS: I understand. I'll be able to read and write in my room.

SARAH: Why did you come to these parts, miss?

MISS ROGERS: I've got a job here, Mrs. Slater.

SARAH: You couldn't get a job where you come from then?

MISS ROGERS: No. I could have gone to Ringwood. That's not too far from Wimborne, but I wanted to live in the north. I wanted something different.

SARAH: That's what's wrong with folks today. Everybody wanting something different. Different things. Different places. Chopping and changing. Why can't they leave things alone?
(MISS ROGERS, eating, does not reply)
Well, I suppose I'll have to clear the table and get on with the washing up. You can come and sit in the kitchen later on.
(Rises and collects most of the dishes)
You might as well have that last bit of pie. I made enough for three, and Jud didn't have much. I was that sure we'd get somebody today.
(Goes to door up right, turns as she opens it)
And there you are. We did, didn't we?

(Blackout)

Scene 3: Blanket Fair

MISS ROGERS, bedjacket draped around her shoulders, sits upright in the single bed. She has a briefcase in front of her, which she is using as a writing desk. SARAH enters upstage and walks as though through rooms to the double bed. JUD follows a few steps behind. SARAH goes to the left of the bed and starts to undress as she talks. She takes off her shoes and stockings and dress, drapes them over the chair and gets into bed. JUD sits in chair to right of the bed and slowly unlaces his boots.

SARAH: Did you go to the back?

JUD: Ay.

SARAH: I don't want you getting up through the night.
(Gets into bed)
Blanket Fair at last. We've earned it.
(A moment's silence)
I say we've earned it.

JUD: Ay.

MISS ROGERS: (As she writes)
I'm glad I came north. It was a difficult choice. Ringwood is so nice, the people so clean and well behaved. If I had taken that job I would prolly have lived there contentedly all my life. I don't think I will live here all my life. It is like a foreign country. But what are foreign countries for if not to visit?

JUD: (Lets boots fall, but does nothing further to get ready for bed)
Yon lass went to bed early.

SARAH: She was tired. Dorset must be a long way from here. It's a wonder she could climb into bed the amount of food she put away. She finished off that potato pie.
(Mimics her lodger)
Miss Rogers. Miss Pamela Rogers. Miss Gutsy, more like it.

JUD: She paid for it, didn't she?

SARAH: I hope she doesn't eat like that every day.

JUD: You want her money, but you don't want to feed her, is that it?

SARAH: All I ask is a fair profit.

MISS ROGERS: The people here are very strange. They cut old newspapers up into squares and use these instead of toilet paper.

SARAH: You'll have to send one of your Pakis out to get something for your dinner tomorrow.

JUD: Ay.

MISS ROGERS: Must remember to get toilet paper tomorrow.
(She puts her writing materials into the briefcase, closes it, puts it under the bed, then covers herself completely with the bedclothes)

SARAH: (Turns on her side away from JUD)
Are you going to sit there all night? Come to bed.

JUD: I'll only be a minute.

SARAH: Switch that light off then.
(JUD reaches up as though for a light switch. Blackout)

(The lights rise almost immediately downstage as a male voice is heard off left singing a lively song. JUD's eyes are closed as he sits in the chair. HARRY PLATT enters extreme left. He is about thirty, short and thin, his movements quick and lively. He has an innocent, boyish face. He wears highly polished fancy clogs, khaki trousers and shirt, muffler and old blue serge jacket. Laughter is never very far from his eyes, from his mouth, from his voice. He crosses slowly to the generator, singing softly as he does so. He does a quick little dance then sits in a chair)

HARRY: (Calls) Jud!
(Takes a tin out of his jacket pocket, breaks open a few cigarette ends and rolls two cigarettes, singing softly as he does so)
Where are you, Jud lad?
(JUD opens his eyes, rises slowly, then stands listening. HARRY rises, moves a step or two right, calls)
Jud!
(JUD approaches HARRY as though sleepwalking. When he gets near him he smiles. A small, dreamy, wanting to believe it smile)

JUD: You got here then?

HARRY: I always get here Wakes Week, don't I? You look as though you've seen a ghost.
(Moves one of the chairs a little)
Sit down afore you fall down.
(They both sit down. HARRY hands JUD one of the cigarettes)
Have a smoke. There's the bottom half of a Balkan Sobranie in that. If you're not careful it'll give you gout in your left lung. You'll find yourself coughing with a la-di-da accent.

JUD: (As they light up) I see you've still got your clogs. They didn't take them away from you then?

HARRY: Who'd want to take them away? They're mine for life.

JUD: (The little smile comes and goes)
That's right. They are. I remember when you won 'em. Harry Platt, the champion clog dancer of all Lancashire.

HARRY: I should think you do remember. It's not all that long since.

JUD: That were a grand day. Grand. The sun shone all day. There were Morris dancers as well as the clog dancers.
(The smile comes and goes)
And three colliery bands, turn and turn about. Beer and meat pies and sausage rolls, with tea and fancy cakes for the women and childer. I believe there was a maypole, too. Do you recall it, Harry?

HARRY: (Slips clogs off, leaps to his feet, holds clogs on high)
The best man won, you see. There's fairation after all. I'll ne'er wear owt but these. These'll do me. These 'ud make a cripple dance.

JUD: How they cheered... They stopped having the competitions soon after.

HARRY: (Bewildered) Did they? That's news to me.
(Puts clogs on, does a little dance)
I feel a rare old booze-up coming on, lad. I've been weeks on my own in the Lake District. Water, water everywhere and not a drop of beer. Will she let you out, lad? Will she let you out?

JUD: She always does at Wakes Week.
(A big smile suddenly makes him look younger)
Is it really holiday time again?

HARRY: Of course it is. What's the matter with you? It's the first week in July, isn't it?

JUD: I reckon it must be.

HARRY: It's always holiday time for me.

JUD: It is that. I don't know how you get away with it.

HARRY: It's not that I'm lazy. You know me better than that. I can walk twenty mile non-stop, then dance for me supper.
(Does a little dance)
That's not laziness, Jud.
(Sits)
Do you remember when I did work? When we both started in the spinning room?

JUD: Ay. You worked for Joe Flanagan. He were a mean un. Even for a spinner. You threw a bobbin at him. You marked him for life.

HARRY: Ay. Well, I've regretted it since. He were sick and he had a nagging wife and a lass that went to the bad. He tormented me beyond endurance, though.

(They smoke in silence for a moment)

What happened to Joe Flanagan? I haven't heard of him for years.

JUD: Dead. Drowned dead.

(The smile has gone. It is as though it has never been. He gazes unblinkingly at HARRY)

He threw himself in the cut. They had to drag for him. He were in there three days.

(Rises, stands over HARRY)

When did they let you out? I haven't seen you since they took you to Liverpool.

HARRY: Liverpool? I've never been to Liverpool. I wouldn't be found dead there. Loston's too mucky for me, never mind Liverpool.

JUD: (Looks away) I meant to tell them. I kept putting it off.

HARRY: Tell them? Tell who? What're you on about?

JUD: (Patiently) They took you away. Don't you remember?

(HARRY shakes his head in bewilderment)

They took you to jail.

HARRY: They took me to jail, all right, but not to Liverpool.

(Rises. There is a slight change in the way he speaks. A slight jerkiness around the edges of his jauntiness)

Never Liverpool. Seven days with the option. Fourteen days with the option. When you've got no money what good's the bloody option? Thirty days without the option. No visible means of support. Menace to the community. Bad example to honest working men. Wish we could still transport the likes of you. Six months without the option.

(Hands in pockets, starts to dance)

The only option I've got, my lords and bloody masters, is to work or not to bloody work. And I choose, with malice aforethought, not to bloody work. I choose to walk and dance the miles away.

(Stops dancing)

I choose to hark to birds, not to you lot. Your words have maggots in 'em. You'll happen catch fish with 'em, but you won't catch me. You want to know when I will work? When there's no bloody bosses. When there's no magistrates and no jails.

(Starts to dance again)

The day will come, Jud lad. The day will come when the bosses will be on their knees begging for mercy.

(Kicks as he dances)

HARRY: (CONT'D)
Take that, you bastards. And that... and that.
(His dancing takes him left)
Oh, I'll dance that day. I'll dance my bloody clogs off.
(Goes off left dancing and kicking)

JUD:
Harry?
(Goes left a step or two and stops)
Did they let you wear your clogs?
(Takes another step or two and shouts)
Did they let you wear your clogs?

(MATT SLATER and his wife, TESS, enter through down right door. MATT is a younger, bigger, better looking version of JUD. He is, for the time being, happier than JUD. He wears a good suit, white silk muffler and a cloth cap. The suit would have been reasonably fashionable in the late thirties. TESS is slim and neat. Although more attractive, it is possible to see that she is the mother of SARAH. Perhaps it is her voice, or some movement or mannerism. Her clothing is neat enough for the time and place. They go up to the table. MATT sits, takes his cap off and throws it on to the table. TESS moves indecisively about. She has something on her mind, something that has to be said, but she doesn't know how to begin)

MATT:
How about a cup of tea then?

JUD:
(Still gazing off left)
I'm that sorry, Harry. I'm that sorry.
(Turns and goes slowly right, then up towards the double bed)

MATT:
Tess.
(TESS turns to him)
I fancy a cup of tea, love.
(JUD stops moving as he hears his father's voice. He turns and listens, then moves nearer to them)

TESS:
All right, I'll put the kettle on.
(Moves towards upstage door, turns, goes down, takes her coat off and puts it on one of the chairs)
Matt, I must talk to you.

MATT:
Won't it wait till you've brewed up?

TESS:
No, it won't.
(Goes nearer to him)
It's about our Sarah.

MATT:
(Indifferently) What about our Sarah?

TESS: (The words are forced from her)
She's in trouble.

MATT: Trouble? What sort of trouble?

TESS: Sort of trouble. What sort of trouble do you think? What's the worst trouble a girl can get into?

MATT: (Rises) Are you sure? Did you take her to the doctor?

TESS: I don't need to take her to the doctor. She's well over a month overdue. I tell you she's in trouble. Oh, the shame of it, Matt. Our Sarah!

MATT: Your Sarah. Her's no flesh of mine.

TESS: Our Sarah. You're her father now. She calls you dad. You know she calls you dad.

MATT: Her can call me dad till her tongue drops off, and her by-blow can call me grand-dad, but that doesn't alter the fact that her's no flesh of mine. Her's your family and that fly-by-night first man of yours. It mun be in the blood. Nowt like this e'er happened in my family.

TESS: It's happened in mine then? Is that what you're saying, Matt Slater?

MATT: It's just happened, hasn't it? As to whether it's happened afore I couldn't tell you. You're not from these parts.

TESS: I'll have you know we're all respectable in my family, with every girl wedded afore she was bedded, and every child with its dad's name on it at birth. Oh, the scandal, Matt. I'll never live it down.

MATT: I knew no good would come of all this gadding about. Her's been left on her own too much.

TESS: We never left her on her own. Jud was always here.

MATT: Where is she?

TESS: In her room, crying her heart out.

MATT: Did she say who she opened her legs for?

TESS: I can't get a word out of her. She's done nothing but cry all day.

MATT: I'll give her something to cry about if she doesn't let on who did it. You're to blame as much as she is. Christ, her's only just fourteen.

(Unbuckles his belt)

Bring her down here.

TESS: What are you going to do? You mustn't chastise her. Not today, Matt.

MATT: I mun find out who it were. I'll leather her if I have to.

TESS: No, Matt.

MATT: (Takes off his belt)

Bring her down.

(TESS goes quickly to upstage door and opens it. YOUNG SARAH stands there in her nightdress. She is plump and would be pretty but for her dishevelled hair and tear stained face. TESS takes her by the hand. They go slowly down to MATT. JUD stands motionless watching them. As they get near to MATT, YOUNG SARAH lets go of her mother's hand and crouches on the floor. MATT takes a step towards her)

Who did it then? Tell us who did it.

YOUNG SARAH: (Sobs) Nobody. It were nobody.

MATT: What are you carrying then, a bloody Jesus? Who were it?

YOUNG SARAH: I won't tell you. I won't. I won't.

MATT: You'll tell me, Sarah, do you hear? I mun know. I'll leather you till the blood comes if I have to, but I mun know. Then I'll leather him till he begs for mercy, but he'll get no mercy from me. I'll geld the bugger. Who were it?

YOUNG SARAH: Nobody... Nobody.

MATT: (Threatens with belt) Who were it?

TESS: Don't, Matt. Don't. What good will that do?

MATT: (Raises belt) Who were it?

(JUD suddenly breaks out of his near trance. He runs and grabs his father's arm)

JUD: Stop it! Stop it, our dad. I know who it were.

MATT: (Dawning fear in his eyes) Tha knows, Jud?

JUD: Ay.

MATT: Who were it then?

JUD: Me. It were me, dad.

MATT: (Lets belt fall as he slumps down at the table)
Thee, Jud?
(MATT, TESS and YOUNG SARAH freeze in their positions as JUD moves away and crosses to the double bed. He sits in the chair. His eyes close)

JUD: It finished my dad. Finished him.
(His eyes open. He gets slowly to his feet. He stamps his foot on the floor. And again)
Pins and bloody needles again. There must be something wrong with my circulation.
(The lights begin to dim as he takes off his shirt and trousers and gets into bed)
I'd have a check-up only all the doctors hereabouts are Pakis. What do they know about the likes of us?
(JUD is in bed now, lying stiff and desolate as far as he can get from SARAH. The lights are very low, almost off)
It finished all of us. All finished. All done.
(The lights are off now. There is silence for a moment or two, then a sudden, strangled screamshout)
FORGIVE ME!
(A spot picks out MISS ROGERS as she sits bolt upright in bed listening to the sudden silence)

END OF ACT I

ACT II

Scene 4: The Graveyard

As Scene 1. JUD prostrate on the grave. SARAH stands implacable to the right.

SARAH: Pray!

JUD: (Goes back on his knees) Our Father, forgive us--

SARAH: Forgive you, our Jud. Forgive you.

JUD: Our Father which art in Heaven hallowed by thy name for ever and ever only forgive me.

SARAH: He won't forgive you.

JUD: (Tries to tear the earth apart, to roll back the sod and bring the bones to the sun again)
I were mad. I were mad. Forgive me, our Nellie, forgive me.

SARAH: She won't forgive you.

JUD: Her will. Her'll forgive me.

SARAH: Not her, Jud. Not our Nellie.

JUD: Her'll forgive me.

SARAH: What about Harry Platt then? He won't forgive you.

JUD: Oh my Christ Harry I meant to tell them. I kept putting it off. I didn't know how to go about it, like. Then it were too late.

SARAH: Ask him then. Ask him.

JUD: I'm sorry, Harry. Forgive me then.

SARAH: He won't. He won't.

JUD: You don't know Harry like I do.

SARAH: There's only one who'll forgive you. You know that.
(After a moment)
Who'll forgive you then?
(JUD raises his head and stares blankly at her)
Who'll forgive you?

JUD: (Almost in a whisper) You, Sarah.

SARAH: Who else?

JUD: None else, Sarah. Only you.

SARAH: Why then? Why will I forgive you?

JUD: (The words are squeezed from him)
Because you love me. Because you love your Jud.

SARAH: And?

JUD: (The words almost choke him)
And... and I love you, Sarah.

(Blackout)

Scene 5: Settling In

The vases have disappeared. The scrim rises as SARAH enters upstage. She has an apron on over her black dress and is carrying a pan. She goes down to the table with it. The table is set for three.

SARAH: (Puts pan on table, talks fretfully to herself)
What's keeping him? (Takes lid off pan, puts it back on)
He's not stuck in that shed, is he?
(SARAH goes up and off through upstage door. JUD enters down left wheeling his bicycle. He leans bicycle against the generator. MISS ROGERS' bicycle leans against the other side of it. He takes his cap off and scratches his head, then crosses right, using extreme downstage area to do so. He goes through down right door, takes off his jacket and muffler and hangs these, together with his cap, behind the door. He goes up to the table as SARAH enters carrying a pan. As she goes down to table:)
There you are then. And not before time.
(Puts pan on table)
Do you know what you did? You locked that shed door again with Miss Gutsy's bike inside. What's ailing you? That's the second time you've done that. I'd like to know what you've got in that shed that you have to keep it locked up all the time.

JUD: (Sits) My mind must have been on something else. Is tea ready then?

SARAH: (Ladles food on to two of the plates)
It's been ready for the past half hour. It was all I could do to keep it from drying up. What kept you so long?

JUD: I had to splice a belt. Last minute job.

SARAH: (Pours tea) Couldn't whatshisname do it?

JUD: Who, Ali? If I'd left it to him he'd still have been at it when the afternoon shift went home.

SARAH: (Sits) You leave her bike outside that shed tomorrow, do you hear?

JUD: I've had a hard day, Sarah. Let me be.

SARAH: If she loses her job it'll be your fault.

JUD: (Starts to eat) I don't want to hear another word about that bloody bike.

SARAH: (Starts to eat) Language, Jud Slater. You're not with your Pakis now. There'll be no swearing in this house while Miss Gutsy's here. She's a cut or two above us and don't you forget it.

JUD: We'll all be equal when we're under the sod. The sod's a great leveller.

SARAH: What's the sod to do with it? We're a long way from the sod yet.
(Silence but for the chomping, the long swallows of tea)
It'll be a wonder if she doesn't get sacked. She must have been an hour late this morning. There's no bus this side of Chapel Street, and you only get one along there when the driver wants a change.
(MISS ROGERS enters downstage left, crosses to down right door, goes through, across and up to the single bed. She takes her coat off and drapes it across the chair)

JUD: They'll keep her on. Schoolteaching's not the same as working for a living.

SARAH: It's taking her long enough.

JUD: It's a fair walk from yon school.

SARAH: Yon's her. (Calls) Come and have your tea, miss.

MISS ROGERS: (Calls) Just a minute.
(Looks around for a moment, then goes over to the table)

SARAH: Sit down then.

MISS ROGERS: (Sits) Sorry I'm late.

SARAH: It's Jud that should be sorry. Say you're sorry, Jud.

MISS ROGERS: Oh, that's all right, Mrs. Slater. I can understand him forgetting that the bicycle was in there.

SARAH: (Ladles out food, passes it to Miss Rogers)
He's to say he's sorry, miss.

MISS ROGERS: It really doesn't matter.

JUD: I am sorry, miss. I've locked that door so often as I do it without thinking about it.

MISS ROGERS: (Starts to eat) It's quite all right, Mr. Slater. As it happened my first class wasn't until ten o'clock.

SARAH: Hot pot again, I'm afraid. But there, it's Monday. What else is there to make on Monday but hot pot?

MISS ROGERS: It's very good... I'm even getting used to sloppy peas.

SARAH: They won't do you any harm.

JUD: I'll see it doesn't happen again, miss. I swear I'll put your bike out for you every morning. I'll keep it clean, too. Mend punctures and that. I'm champion at fixing things. I've had Flossie upwards of twenty year. Many's the time something's gone wrong, but I've always fixed it myself.

SARAH: We don't want to hear about Flossie, Jud.
(Silence but for the sounds of eating and drinking)

MISS ROGERS: I'll be quite late for tea tomorrow. I may spend an hour or two in the library. Things like that. You have a very nice new library.

SARAH: Have we? I've ne'er seen it.

MISS ROGERS: You must have. It's near the market place .

SARAH: I'll take your word for it, miss, but I've ne'er seen it.
(Silence again)
I'll leave your tea on the hob tomorrow then. It won't be my fault if it dries up.

MISS ROGERS: I'm sure it will be all right.

SARAH: You're settling in at the school then?

MISS ROGERS: More or less... I find it difficult to get to know some of the children, though.

SARAH: You're new. They'll be sizing you up.

MISS ROGERS: Everybody's new, Mrs. Slater. It's a new school.

SARAH: They didn't have art in our time. Art wasn't for the likes of us.

MISS ROGERS: Wasn't it? What did you have?

SARAH: Reading, writing, sums and the strap.

JUD: Don't forget the kings and bloody queens. They dinned all the kings and bloody queens into us as well.

SARAH: Language, Jud.
(JUD takes a long swallow of tea, slams the mug down, rises and goes down left)

SARAH: Where are you off to then?

JUD: (As he moves away) I'm off to yon shed. I can say what I like there.
(Sits near the generator, lights cigarette)

SARAH: But you haven't had your rice pudding.
(After a moment)
I don't know what's getting into him these days. He must be working too hard.

MISS ROGERS: Is his job very hard? What does he actually do?

SARAH: Have you ever been in a spinning room?

MISS ROGERS: Of course not.

SARAH: It wouldn't be much use me telling you what he does then, would it?

(Blackout)

Scene 6: A Little Chat

JUD sits by the generator, the bit of rag in his hand. He gently and automatically wipes the housing.

JUD: Her's bound to get home soon. That library must be shut by now.

(Rises, goes left and gazes off, goes back to the generator)

She must be lonely here, Flossie. All alone and far from home.

(Wipes the seat of one of the chairs)

She can sit in this. I'm sure Harry won't mind. A little chat might cheer her up. To tell you the truth I'm lonely, too. I'm that lonely. Who is there I can have a laugh and a chinwag with? It wasn't always like this. There wasn't just Harry. It's not right.

(JUD turns his head, listening. He goes quickly left and stands waiting. MISS ROGERS enters wheeling her bicycle. She is a little out of breath and stands for a moment breathing deeply. JUD stands looking at her unmoving and unblinking)

MISS ROGERS: Good evening, Mr. Slater.

JUD: (Moves suddenly and quickly)

Here, let me take that.

(Takes bicycle from her, wheels it right and leans it against the generator)

Come in then, lass.

MISS ROGERS: (Approaches) I really must go and get my tea. I've very hungry.

JUD: You can come in for a minute. Your tea won't go away.

MISS ROGERS: (Comes a little nearer, imitates SARAH's voice)

No, but it might dry up.

JUD: (Goes along with her)

It won't be my fault if it does.

(There are two books in the carrier of the bicycle. He picks one of them up)

Remembrance of Things Past.

(Puts it back in the carrier)

That wouldn't do me much good.

MISS ROGERS: (Smiles) Why not?

JUD: It's the forgetting of things past that would do the trick for me... Come in then.

(MISS ROGERS moves nearer to the generator)

I don't believe you've met Flossie.

MISS ROGERS: No. You always keep this place locked.

JUD: Keeps her out. Her's never been in here.

MISS ROGERS: (Moves a little closer)
So this is Flossie.

JUD: Ay. This here's Miss Rogers, Floss. A schoolteacher, no less. We are going up in the world, aren't we?
(MISS ROGERS turns to go)
Don't go, lass.
(Moves a chair a little nearer to her)
Sit thee down.

MISS ROGERS: (Sits) I really must get something to eat soon.

JUD: That's Harry's chair. Nobody's sat in that for a long time.
(Sits, looks around appreciatively)
This is my sanctum sanctorum. You're welcome to pay me a visit whenever you like, though.

MISS ROGERS: Sanctum sanctorum means holy of holies. Is this really your holy of holies?

JUD: Is that what it means, lass? I didn't know. It's just something I read somewhere.

MISS ROGERS: I'm hungry. I didn't have much lunch. Mrs. Slater makes such heavy meals that I'll put weight on if I don't cut down on lunches. How do you keep so thin?

JUD: I've done no but fret and work hard all me life. That tends to fine a man down.

MISS ROGERS: (Unfastens her coat) Don't you think it's too warm in here, Mr. Slater?

JUD: I'm used to more warmth than this in yon spinning room. Flossie likes it warm, don't you, Floss?... Harry liked it warm, too. "You can't have it too warm for me", he used to say. Sitting in that very chair he used to say that, with the steam rising off him. He'd likely have walked twenty mile or more in the cold and rain to get here.
(Turns his unblinking gaze on her)
Harry's dead, you know. He were my best friend. We spent every Wakes week together. He were a tramp, and a rare un. He could dance the miles away. He weren't the size o' sixpennorth o' copper when he broke Joe Flannagan's head with a bobbin and ran off. He never did a hand's turn o' work after that. Not a hand's turn. Joe Flannagan were his spinner. He were too hard on little Harry.

MISS ROGERS: (At a loss) What did he die of?
(JUD gazes unblinkingly at her)
Was it exposure?
(No answer)
Was it an accident?

JUD: It were no accident.
(Turns head away, his hand goes to his top teeth)
They hung him. No, you couldn't call that an accident. They set out to do it. He were a tramp, so they hung him.

MISS ROGERS: You must be wrong, Mr. Slater. They don't hang people in England just because they are tramps.

JUD: (Turns his blank, lost gaze on her)
They don't hang anybody at all now. They just put them away. This were a long time ago. They hung him twenty year ago and more. They said he were a sex fiend and a murderer, but I know better. Harry Platt ne'er hurt a soul but for the time he threw that bobbin at Joe Flannagan, and he were tormented beyond endurance then.

MISS ROGERS: Who was it that was murdered? Was it somebody you knew?

JUD: (Tonelessly) Ay. I knew her.

MISS ROGERS: Did nobody try to help your friend? Did you try to help him?

JUD: I meant to, lass. I swear I meant to. I kept putting it off. Then _she_ stopped me. She said he were bound to get off. It were easy to believe her. I wanted to, you see. Then it were too late. I wonder how many folk have been hung because they had no home and nobody to speak up for them.

MISS ROGERS: Not many, I'm sure. Not in England. There's law and justice in England.

JUD: Is there, lass? Then how is it that the only man I ever knew that was hung was a homeless tramp who had nobody to speak up for him?
(Rises, raises his voice)
I tell you Harry didn't do it. He were miles away. He told them he were miles away. They didn't believe him. He couldn't prove it, you see. They didn't want to believe him. It would have meant they'd done all that work for nothing. They had to hang somebody. Harry were handy, and, as I say, with nobody to speak up for him.
(Moves away)
I should have spoke up. I meant to. I swear I meant to.

MISS ROGERS: Could you really have helped him?

JUD: <u>She</u> talked me out of it. She said they'd never hang him. But they did. They hung him there in Liverpool, and I ne'er saw him again. He did his last dance on air, with strangers watching and happen gloating.
(Moves near MISS ROGERS)
Her's my step-sister, you know.

MISS ROGERS: (Rises) I must have something to eat.

JUD: My dad married her mother.

MISS ROGERS: (Moves away down right)
You mustn't blame yourself, Mr. Slater.
(Turns, goes back to her bicycle, takes books out of carrier)
After all, it seems that nobody else helped him.

JUD: Her were that bonny once. She swore they wouldn't hang him.

MISS ROGERS: You must stop going over it in your mind.
(Moves away right and turns)
You must try to forget.
(SARAH enters upstage, goes down beyond table and stands looking left)

JUD: It's funny. I do forget sometimes. Don't go, lass.

MISS ROGERS: I must.

JUD: You could happen help me. Come and visit every so oft. Sit in Harry's chair and have a chinwag. There's no harm in that, is there?

MISS ROGERS: Of course not. I'll drop in for a chat now and again. I must go now.
(Mimics SARAH)
That tea'll be dried up.
(Crosses extreme downstage to stage right door)

JUD: (His hand goes to his mouth, pushes up on his top teeth)
They'd have let him off if I'd spoke up. You'd have danced away into the fields, Harry, not down into that unmarked grave... I mun get away.
(Goes to generator, automatically wipes the housing)
Do you hear me, Floss? I mun get away.
(Sits and holds head in his hands as MISS ROGERS goes through the door and across up towards the single bed)

SARAH: (Calls) I want a word with you, miss.

MISS ROGERS: (Carries on towards the bed)
I'll be there in a minute, Mrs. Slater.

SARAH: You'll come here now.

MISS ROGERS: (Approaches SARAH) What is it?

SARAH: I saw you coming out of that shed just now.

MISS ROGERS: Yes? I put my bicycle away and stopped to talk to Mr. Slater.

SARAH: You keep out of that shed in future, miss. He's not much to look at, but he's my man.

MISS ROGERS: (Goes a little nearer to SARAH)
Your...your man. You surely don't think... Oh, you couldn't think that.

SARAH: It's no matter what I think. I've never been in that shed.

MISS ROGERS: I didn't want to go into the filthy place. I had to put my bicycle in there.

SARAH: It's out of bounds to me, so it should be out of bounds to you. I want your solemn promise you won't go in there again.

MISS ROGERS: Your husband has things on his mind, Mrs. Slater. He wanted to talk about them, so I let him talk.

SARAH: If he wants to talk to somebody he can talk to me. I know what ails him. You leave my man alone.

MISS ROGERS: All right.
(As she turns and goes towards the bed)
I will leave as soon as I can find another room. I'll start looking for one tomorrow.

SARAH: There's no harm in looking, miss. Finding is something else again.

MISS ROGERS: I'll find a room, Mrs. Slater.

SARAH: You'll give a full week's notice when you do. You'll pay me the full six pounds.
(Calls after a moment)
What about your tea then?

MISS ROGERS: (Throws her coat on the bed, sits and opens one of the books)
I don't want any tea.

(SARAH goes quickly to upstage door and off, enters almost immediately carrying a plate of food)

SARAH: Jud!

JUD: (Wearily) What is it now?

SARAH: (Puts plate on table)
You come in here... I don't want any tea. Don't you then? You'll eat it soon enough, and you'll eat it cold... Jud!

JUD: (Stands in down right doorway)
What is it then? Do you have to shout like that? What will yon lodger think?

SARAH: She'll happen think it's not so very quiet here after all. Are you going to stand there with that door open all night?

JUD: (Closes door, stands with his back to it)
Does that suit you?

SARAH: What were you doing in that shed with Miss Gutsy?

JUD: (Approaches table) We had a little chat, Sarah. Just a little chat.

SARAH: There'll be no more little chats. Flossie I don't mind, but you'll leave that girl alone.

JUD: (Sits) Is this her tea? It'll get cold.

SARAH: Let it. She's going to look for another room tomorrow. Fat chance she's got of finding one. You see what happens when you start your little chats?

JUD: Did I upset her then?

SARAH: You keep away from her in future.

JUD: Who is there that I know? Who is there that I can sit down and have a chinwag with?

SARAH: Do I know anybody then?

JUD: All the folk there are in the world, and how many do you think I know? I'll tell you in one word. None. N-o-bloody-n-e. None.

SARAH: (Sits) Whose fault's that then?

JUD: I know old Horrocks at the mill. He talks to me. He lays down the law. And I talk right back at him. "Yes, Mr. Horrocks." "No, Mr. Horrocks." "That's right, Mr. Horrocks." Very entertaining. I get a laugh out of him once a year regular.

SARAH: Do I talk to anybody then? Have I got a fancy man with a silver tongue hidden away in that kitchen?

JUD: I know a few Pakis, too. They quite often say "Good morning" to me, and "Yes, Jud", and "No, Jud", and "That's right, Jud".

SARAH: I don't even know any Pakis.

JUD: I've been hard done by. I mun get away. Let me go, Sarah. Let me go. It's not too late for me to start afresh. Look at Charlie Chaplin. He married a young un when he were past my age.

SARAH: Charlie Chaplin could afford to marry young un.

JUD: I'd be better off if I were a Paki. I swear to God I would. All this because you enticed me.

SARAH: I didn't entice you. You couldn't keep your hands off me. You were after me morning, noon and night. You gave me no peace till you had your way.
(Picks up the plate of food)
Shall I put this back on the hob, do you think?
(Puts it back on the table, imitates MISS ROGERS)
I'll look for another room tomorrow... All because I told her to keep out of that shed. I'm not allowed in there. Why should she be?

JUD: (Rises) Have you been on to her then? I thought it were something I'd said.
(Goes right and calls)
Miss...
(MISS ROGERS puts her book down)
We'd like to see you in the parlour, miss, if you don't mind. Is that tea warm enough?

SARAH: It's warm enough for her.

JUD: (Approaches her) Now you listen to me for a change. I asked her in that shed. Her were good enough to sit and listen to me. You'll say you're sorry and you'll ask her to stay. You want the money and I want the company. When she comes down you'll make her welcome and say you're sorry. She gets little enough for her six pounds a week as it is.

SARAH: I'll do no such thing.
(MISS ROGERS slowly crosses towards table)

JUD: Won't you? I'm getting to the state when I don't care what happens to me. Do you understand? If need be I'll make an end of it all. You'll make her welcome and you'll say you're sorry... Come in, lass. Come in and have your tea. Sarah's sorry for what she said. Aren't you, Sarah?

SARAH: (Moves things around on the table)
I shouldn't have said what I did, miss.

JUD: And you're sorry you said it.

SARAH: I'm sorry then... It's not my fault if your tea's not what it should be. It were cooked hours ago.

JUD: Sit thee down, lass.

MISS ROGERS: (Sits) Thank you.

JUD: Are we still friends then?

MISS ROGERS: Friends? Well, I suppose we can keep our relationship as it was before...before this happened.

SARAH: Steak puddings should be eaten as soon as they're cooked. They get heavy, like.

MISS ROGERS: I'm sure it will be all right.

JUD: That'll stick to your insides, all right... You'll stay with us for a while then?

MISS ROGERS: (Starts to eat) It may take me a few weeks to find a decent room, but I _am_ going to look for one.

JUD: You won't leave over what Sarah said, though?

MISS ROGERS: No. It's quite all right, Mrs. Slater. I won't go in the shed again.

SARAH: I shouldn't have said what I did.

JUD: We'll let the lass have a bit o' peace over her tea.
(Goes up towards the door)
Come on, Sarah.

SARAH: (Goes up as JUD opens the door)
Good night then, miss.

JUD: (As SARAH goes off) Good night, lass... You'll happen stay till Xmas then?

MISS ROGERS: Perhaps. (With a tiny smile) Yes, probably till Xmas. (Opens her book) Good night, Mr. Slater.

(Blackout)

Scene 7: Remembrance of Things Past

JUD stands in front of the lectern. He turns a page or two, then slams the book shut.

JUD: Sarah!... Come in here, our Sarah.
(His hand traces OUR BABY on the book)
Sarah!
(Goes to upstage door, opens it)
Sarah!

SARAH: (Off) What is it then?

JUD: Come in here.
(Leaves door open, goes down to lectern, opens book)

SARAH: (In doorway) You keep away from that book.
(Closes door and goes up to him)
She was my baby and it's my book.

JUD: Our baby. OUR BABY's written on it as plain as day.
(His hand traces the lettering)
It couldn't be plainer than that, could it?

SARAH: They didn't have any that said my baby. What ails you then? I were nodding by the fire.

JUD: (Moves away from her, goes to table and pulls out a chair)
Sit down, Sarah. Happen we can talk things over.

SARAH: (Moves down to him) Talk things over? Are you sickening for something, Jud?

JUD: (Tauntingly) How long is it since?

SARAH: (Uneasily) How long is it since what?
(Sits)
I'm blessed if I know what you're talking about. Aren't you going to sit down?

JUD: I asked you a question, Sarah.

SARAH: I've no idea what you're talking about.

JUD: You know all right.
(Bends over her)
How long is it since?

SARAH: (Defiantly) I'm sure I don't know. I don't keep a tally.

JUD: A tally! You wouldn't need much pencil and paper if you did. (Moves away from her) It's upwards of ten years since.
(SARAH suddenly covers her face with her apron and rocks in the chair. When she uncovers her face her eyes are closed, her voice is a monotone)

SARAH: Who do you love then? Say who you love.

JUD: I'll not. Do you understand? I'll bloody not. I'm at the end of my tether.

SARAH: (Opens her eyes, her voice is harsh)
What about me, then? Night after night in the same bed with a man who isn't a man.

JUD: We're past it now, Sarah.

SARAH: I'm not past it.

JUD: You might not be past it in yourself, Sarah, but you're past it as far as anybody else is concerned.

SARAH: Have I changed that much then?'

JUD: We've all changed.

SARAH: I were bonny once, weren't I?

JUD: Ay. You were that bonny.

SARAH: Our Nellie were lovely. She must have got it from somewhere. I must have been bonny. You followed me around for months till you had your way that first time. Whenever I turned round there you were. Do you remember, Jud?

JUD: Ay.
(Goes down to her)
We only did it once then. Only once proper and you had one up the spout right off. (Without inflection) To tell you the truth I didn't enjoy it. I were too fright they'd come in and catch us at it.

SARAH: Do you think I enjoyed it then?

JUD: Them magistrates. They carried on as though we'd been caught doing a Guy Fawkes. They give 'em a bloody medal and a council house now for doing what we did.

SARAH: Times have changed out there. The telly. Motor cars. Aeroplanes. Rockets. Do they do all that dashing about just to get more things, Jud?

JUD: (Sits) They're all daft.

SARAH: All bar us. Money in the bank. I were sure Miss Gutsy would be here till the school breaks up for the summer holidays. I had it all reckoned up, and now she's looking for another room. I should have known better. Nothing's sure in this world.

JUD: There's some things sure. There's the sod and yon factory whistle. That'll blow in the morning. You see if it doesn't.

SARAH: You get used to the money coming in regular. You get used to a good lodger. Then she goes and the money stops coming in.

JUD: We don't need the money.

SARAH: I need it. I need the comfort of it. I like to see the money going in. I like to see them write it down. I hate taking it out.

JUD: Leave it in then.

SARAH: We're bound to get somebody. We'll be all right.

JUD: We're all right now.

SARAH: You speak for yourself. You have your Pakis. You have Flossie. I've got the walk to the bank every Monday morn. When there's no lodger's money it's hardly worth it. They look down their noses at me when there's no lodger's money. They don't want dribs and drabs. They want it in handfuls. That's the way they are in banks.

JUD: Money's naught to me.

SARAH: It's a good job it's something to me then. You'd soon go under without money. You'd soon be on the Parish.

JUD: There's no Parish now. It's the Social Security.

SARAH: They've given it a different name, but it's still the Parish. They can call a workhouse a hospital if they like, but it's still a workhouse to the likes of us. Would you like to end your days in a workhouse then?

JUD: I sometimes think I'd just like to end my days.
(Goes up to lectern)
There mun be a way out.
(Pounds with his fist on the scrapbook)
If I got away I could happen forget. I could be myself again.
(Picks up scrapbook)
I should start by burning this.

SARAH: (Rises quickly) Leave my book alone.
(Goes up, snatches book from JUD)
She were _my_ baby.

JUD: _Ours_.

SARAH: _I_ bore her.

JUD: (Moves away) This isn't what I wanted to talk about.
I'm off to yon shed.

SARAH: (Harshly) You'll stay where you are.
(JUD, near table, stands motionless, unblinking eyes fixed straight ahead)
Her were that bonny.
(Suddenly raises scrapbook at arms height above her)
On your knees, Jud Slater.

JUD: (Eyes still fixed away from her)
Nay, I'll not.

SARAH: On your _knees_.
(MISS ROGERS enters extreme downstage left carrying a folded easel. She walks across and to the down right door)

JUD: (Slumps to his knees) Oh my holy roasting suffering crucified Jesus bloody Christ. Is there to be no end to it?

SARAH: Pray.

JUD: I'll not pray. This isn't yon graveyard.
(MISS ROGERS goes through down right door, then goes left and up)

SARAH: Graveyard or not you'll pray.

MISS ROGERS: (Starts to speak before becoming aware of the oddness of the tableau before her)
I'm going into town, Mr. Slater. I'll need --

JUD: (Looks up at SARAH) I tell thee I'll not.

MISS ROGERS: (Stopped dead in her tracks) --my bicycle.

SARAH: You won't get away with it that easy. What are you then?

MISS ROGERS: Mr. Slater.
(JUD turns his head. SARAH stands motionless, book raised above her)

SARAH: Say what you are.

JUD: (Softly) Yon lass is here.

SARAH: (Turns, the book is brought slowly down and cradled in her arms)
What is it then? Up you get, Jud.
(JUD gets to his feet. SARAH gently rocks the book)

MISS ROGERS: I'm going into town. I'll need my bicycle.
(MISS ROGERS turns and crosses to the single bed. She puts the easel under the bed, then goes slowly across and down and waits restlessly near the generator)

JUD: What shall I tell her then?

SARAH: (Eyes lowered as she gently rocks the book)
Tell her to mind her own business.

JUD: (Moves left) She'll happen start the gossip going again.

SARAH: (Softly as she rocks the book)
Tell her it was a game we were playing then.

JUD: (Goes down and across to MISS ROGERS)
Ay... You're off out again then? It's not a bad day for a ride.

MISS ROGERS: (Embarrassed) I'm going into town. I have an appointment.

JUD: Sarah has her odd ways. You mustn't take any notice. It's water off a duck's back with me.
(Gets her bicycle and wheels it to her)

MISS ROGERS: I'm not sure if I understand you.

JUD: I cleaned and oiled it for you.
(MISS ROGERS takes the bicycle)
She were very fond of our Nellie. It gets too much for her at times. It's like a game she plays. I play along with her to keep the peace. You mustn't let it bother you. I'd be obliged if you wouldn't let on to anybody about it.

MISS ROGERS: I understand. I'll have to hurry now, or I'll be late for my appointment.
(Wheels bicycle left, then stops)
The appointment is with a Mrs. Houghton. Do you know anything about her?

JUD: There'll be more than one Mrs. Houghton hereabouts, lass.

MISS ROGERS: She seems to be very rich. She needs a tutor for her daughter. Part time. She's offering room and board in exchange.

JUD: Good luck then.

MISS ROGERS: Good luck? If the daughter and I hit it off it means that I'll be leaving you soon.

JUD: I still wish you luck, lass.

MISS ROGERS: I'll let you know how things go with Mrs. Houghton. And her daughter, who may be a little beast. (Turns to go)

JUD: You'll be here for Xmas, won't you, lass?

MISS ROGERS: (As she exits) I'm afraid not. Even if I don't get another room I'll be away for Xmas. I always spend Xmas with my parents.

JUD: (Gazes after her) Do you, lass? I didn't know.
(JUD goes slowly across and up to SARAH, who now stands near the lectern with the book still cradled in her arms. She rocks it gently as she speaks)

SARAH: Hush then... Wilta not hush?
(Holds book in both hands away from her)
Was there ever such a bonny babby?
(Clasps book to her breast)
They'll not take thee away from me.
(Cradles book)
They'll not... They'll not.
(Gently rocks book)
Hush then.

JUD: (Approaches her) You can put the book back now, Sarah.

SARAH: It's my book.

JUD: Put it back then.

SARAH: (Changes suddenly) I'll put it back.
(Slams book on to lectern, keeps her hand on it)
I'll put it back, Jud.

JUD: Yon lass has gone to see about another room.

SARAH: Has she then? You should have let the air out of her tires. Didn't you think of that?

JUD: I wished her luck.

SARAH: Luck. Her luck won't do us any good.

JUD: Her's a bonny lass. She deserves better than this.

SARAH: (Opens scrapbook) She would have been bonnier. Look what she got.

JUD: Don't start that again. I've had enough.

SARAH: (Turns a page) Here she is, age two and a bit. At our wedding. They'd let us out the day before.
(JUD moves away, then stands as though caught in a snare. SARAH turns another page)
After the wedding. She's not a by-blow now. There's her dad holding her to prove it. Come and look, her dad.

JUD: I tell thee I've had enough.

SARAH: (Turns page) Age three. Take Nellie walkies, Dadda. (Tauntingly) She has a ribbon in her hair. (Turns page) She's five here.

JUD: (Doesn't move) I used to take her along the cut. (Desperately) I were only nineteen when she were five.

SARAH: (Turns page) Bathtime, Nell. In you go. Oh, isn't she lovely?
(JUD moves as though in a trance and stands with SARAH)
Look, she's smiling at her granny. She loves her granny, don't you, Nell? Don't sit there grieving, mam...Oh, just look at her. I could eat her all up.
(JUD, face expressionless, turns a page)
This was taken at school. Standard three. That's her in the middle of the front row, next to Sister Teresa.

JUD: (Turns page) I know when it were taken, and I know which is our Nellie.

SARAH: She's nine there. That were taken on walking day. Just look at that sash and the white gloves.

JUD: (Turns pages quickly) We're coming to it, Sarah. We're coming to it.

SARAH: She's twelve there. Twelve.
(JUD suddenly moves away. As he moves the portrait of "Our Nellie" gradually becomes visible)

JUD: I'm off to yon shed.

SARAH: (Harshly) You stay where you are. (Turns page) Here it is then.
(The portrait of "Our Nellie" is now fully visible. JUD stands motionless. SARAH raises her voice)
Body found... Schoolgirl murdered... Police hunt sex fiend.
(JUD moves quickly, goes up to her and tries to close the book)
Leave my book alone. That was the "Mirror". Shall I read what the "Express" said? Tragedy hits lonely, happy home. (Tauntingly) You didn't know we were happy, did you, Jud?... Massive manhunt... Innocent girl's last walk through fields on page six. (Turns page) "Mirror" again. Sex murder.
(The portrait of HARRY PLATT gradually becomes visible)
Tramp held for questioning. Here's Harry... Don't you want to look at Harry then?
(The portrait of laughing HARRY PLATT is now fully visible)

JUD: Let me be. I've been hard done by. I mun get away, do you hear?

SARAH: He didn't laugh for very long after that, did he?

JUD: It wasn't right what they did.

SARAH: What they did!

JUD: Poor Harry.

SARAH: Poor Harry!

JUD: Why couldn't you prove where you were? Why did you have to spend days together talking to naught but birds and trees?

SARAH: Poor Harry! What about our Nellie then? What about me?

JUD: They hung Harry Platt.

SARAH: They hung him. He were a child, too, for all his years. Suffer to come unto me, little children. Suffer, Jud.

JUD: Let me be. I swear I've paid.

SARAH: (Approaches him) On your knees, Jud Slater.

JUD: Not again. For Christ's sake not again.

SARAH: On your knees.

JUD: (Slumps to his knees) All right then.

SARAH: What are you? (No answer) Say what you are.

JUD: (By rote) A beast, Sarah. A beast of the fields.

SARAH: Lick my shoes.

JUD: Give us some peace. For Christ's sake give us some peace.

SARAH: Lick my shoes.
(JUD crouches lower and carefully licks each shoe)

SARAH: That'll do.
(JUD goes back on his knees)
Go on then. Say it.

JUD: (By rote) You're the one for me, Sarah. Only you.

SARAH: Say it all then.

JUD: I'm dirty. Filthy rotten dirty.

SARAH: Not that. (JUD looks up at her, eyes blank) I'm waiting.

JUD: We're all waiting, Sarah.

SARAH: Why do you love me? Say it.

JUD: (By rote) You're that bonny, our Sarah.

SARAH: And?

JUD: (Desolately) I mun have you.

SARAH: (A catch to her breath) We mustn't, our Jud. We mustn't.

JUD: (Flatly) Nobody'll know if we don't tell 'em.

SARAH: (Longing in her voice) Oh, Jud, you're a wicked lad. Wicked.

JUD: (Wearily) Have you done?

SARAH: Lick my shoes.
(JUD crouches and carefully licks each shoe)
Are you sorry then?

JUD: (Goes back on his knees) I'm sorry. Christ knows I'm sorry.

SARAH: Will you make it up to me then?

JUD: (Softly) I'll make it up to you, love. I'll work my fingers to the bone.

SARAH: (Moves up towards the lectern) Get up then.
(Closes the book, cradles it in her arms. As SARAH closes the book the portraits fade and vanish)

JUD: (Struggles to his feet) It takes it out of me these days. (Goes up to SARAH) Have you got bunions then?

SARAH: That's not all I've got.

JUD: I noticed you'd cut a bit out of your shoes.

SARAH: You can go now.

JUD: (Doesn't move) Ay.

SARAH: I thought you wanted to go to that shed.

JUD: I do.

SARAH: Off you go then.

JUD: Will you be all right?

SARAH: (Rocks the cradled book) I've got my book, haven't I?

JUD: (Moves away as the lights begin to fade) Ay.

SARAH: (Bends over the book) Hush then... Wilta not hush?

END OF ACT II

ACT III

Scene 8: The Graveyard

As Scene 1. JUD kneels up from the vases. SARAH stands on the right.

SARAH: You grieved your life away, my mam. I'm that sorry. I brought you in tears to this grave. Why didn't you stay with us for a while longer? We needed you. Our Nellie needed you. "Where's Granny?" she kept saying. "Where's Granny?" "Gone to Heaven," I said. "Your Granny's happy at last." Do you know what our Nellie said? "Has she gone by bus?" she said. "Will she have got a return ticket?" I'm sorry, mam. We didn't know what we were doing. I swear we didn't. Look how young we were. You took it hard, mam. You took it too hard.

JUD: (Eyes blank, voice almost without inflection)
Have you done, Sarah? Have you bloody done?

SARAH: (Ignores him) Your dad must be comfy. One wife above. One below. He'll be as snug as the chips in a chip butty.
(Abruptly)
Straighten that vase up.
(JUD moves one of the vases)
That's better. There's nothing nicer than a tidy grave.
(Takes handkerchief from her handbag and wipes her face)
That sun's warm for December. It's all them rockets. Going to the moon. What do they want to tamper with the moon for then? The moon has a lot to do with the weather, I don't care what they say. Flying faster than sound. What for? Where are they all going? Do they do all that dashing about just to get more things, Jud?

JUD: They're all daft.

SARAH: All bar us. Money in the bank. Safe. Walking's good enough for us. Walking never hurt the weather. If they were all like us there'd be no aeroplanes. There'd be no motor cars. All nice and quiet.

JUD: Horses.

SARAH: What's that, Jud?

JUD: I used to like horses. Liked the smell of 'em. Horses never did anybody any harm.

SARAH: (Almost kindly) Get up then.

JUD: (Struggles to his feet, hands brushing ineffectually at his knees)
I'll need a new suit soon.

SARAH: More expense. There's no end to it.
(JUD gazes straight ahead, face expressionless)
Dinner'll be just right when you get home.

JUD: (Moves away) Ay.

SARAH: See you at home then.

JUD: Ay.
(They walk off in opposite directions)

(Blackout)

Scene 9: An Xmas Drink

The vases have disappeared. As the scrim rises JUD is nearing the generator. He carries a small wooden box. He puts it on top of the generator and takes from it a bottle of whiskey, two glasses and a bit of clean white cloth. He then places the box between the two chairs, wipes the glasses, puts the cloth on the box and the bottle of whiskey and glasses on the cloth.

JUD: She couldn't for shame not have a drink with me. Her'll be on edge to get her packing done, ready for an early skedaddle tomorrow. She'll have time for an Xmas drink, though. I bought this for her, Floss. I'd never dream of buying a bottle for myself... Who knows what'll happen when she's got a drink or two inside her... That skin... Them legs.
(Goes down and left a little)
I mun keep an eye out for her. This is our last chance... You can see for miles. Even the cut looks clean with the moon on it... What it must be to drown in water as dirty as that. Poor Joe Flanagan... And all the others. When all turn against you the cut will welcome you. It turns none away.
(Goes a step or two left)

JUD: (CONT'D) Yon must be her. There's somebody coming over the bridge... Cats, dogs, childer, grown ups. Room for all. All taken care of and given the same treatment... That's her all right. She's coming at a fair old lick... There mun be easier ways than the cut. Have a bath, put on a clean shirt, take some sleeping pills, get into bed and wake up dead. No harm to anybody, that. No dragging the cut for hours and hours... That's not a thing to be thinking about with yon lass on her way. Think of her. Her'll be here soon sampling yon whiskey.

(JUD goes back right and waits nearer to the generator. MISS ROGERS enters extreme downstage left wheeling her bicycle. JUD steps forward as she gets near to him. MISS ROGERS stops suddenly)

MISS ROGERS: Is that you, Mr. Slater?

JUD: I didn't frighten you, lass, did I?

MISS ROGERS: It would take a lot to frighten me tonight.

JUD: (Takes bicycle from her) Happy, are you then?

MISS ROGERS: Yes. Isn't it a beautiful night? Aren't you happy, Mr. Slater? It's the Xmas holidays.

JUD: (Wheels bicycle to generator, leans it against it) Not for me. Not yet. We only get two days off, you know. Has your being happy ought to do with leaving us then?

MISS ROGERS: Oh, it's all mixed up with Xmas and everything.

JUD: I have a bottle here.

MISS ROGERS: What's that, Mr. Slater?

JUD: I said I have a bottle here. Whiskey, like. For Xmas.

MISS ROGERS: (At a loss) Have you?

JUD: Ay. I bought it for you.

MISS ROGERS: (Goes nearer to him) For me, Mr. Slater?

JUD: For the two of us then. I was hoping you'd have an Xmas drink with me.

MISS ROGERS: It's very kind of you, but I haven't time. I have to pack. I'm leaving early in the morning.

JUD: Just one drink, lass. For Xmas. I won't keep you long.

MISS ROGERS: I promised Mrs. Slater I wouldn't come in here again.

JUD: That's right, lass. You did.

MISS ROGERS: Oh, all right. I'll do my packing, then come down.

JUD: It would be best to have the drink before you pack. She won't know then... Sit thee down, lass. Use Harry's chair.

MISS ROGERS: (Sits) I can only stay a minute or two.

JUD: (Pours whiskey into the glasses)
We'll see, lass. We'll see. It's good whiskey. I asked for the best. The best they had in the shop. (Hands her a glass, sits) There you are then. Drink up.

MISS ROGERS: Thank you. (Raises glass) Merry Xmas, Mr. Slater.

JUD: Ay. (Does not raise glass) Merry Xmas then.
(They drink and sit in silence for a moment)

MISS ROGERS: It's strong. Don't you think so?

JUD: Ay. But it's smooth, like. Not that I'm any judge of whiskey. Beer's my drink.

MISS ROGERS: Is it? I've never seen any in the house. Do you keep it in here?

JUD: I should have said that when I do drink I drink beer. I hardly ever drink now. There was a time when I'd be down the White Horse or the Red Lion two or three times a week. I used to go down with Harry. That's his chair you're sitting in.

MISS ROGERS: Yes, I know.

JUD: Twenty years have gone by, but I still expect him to come through that door.
(Empties his glass and pours himself another drink)
They hung him, you know.

MISS ROGERS: It's not the kind of thing you should be talking about over an Xmas drink.

JUD: I shouldn't talk about Harry?

MISS ROGERS: Not about hanging. Not at Xmas.

JUD: How can I talk about Harry and not mention the hanging? He was hung.

MISS ROGERS: It's not the thing to talk about now. Christ was born at this time of year. It's a happy time.

JUD: What about Christ then? (Drinks) They hung him, didn't they?

MISS ROGERS: They crucified him.

JUD: That's hanging, isn't it? Not with a rope, but they hung him on a cross, didn't they?

MISS ROGERS: They nailed him to a cross.

JUD: Ay, but he'd be bound to hang there, wouldn't he? From the nails, like?

MISS ROGERS: Let's talk about something else.

JUD: You're nearly done with that drink. I'll top it up for you.

MISS ROGERS: No. I really must go in a minute.

JUD: You've got plenty of time, lass. (Pours whiskey into her glass) Sarah can help with the packing if need be. (Picks up his glass) Merry Xmas then.

MISS ROGERS: (Smiles as she picks up her glass)
Merry Xmas.

JUD: (Empties his glass and pours more whiskey)
You know, lass, he had no home, just like Harry.

MISS ROGERS: Who?

JUD: Christ. He had nobody to speak up for him. They all deserted him, didn't they?

MISS ROGERS: Christ spoke for himself.

JUD: So did Harry. Nobody listened, though... Shall I top your drink up?

MISS ROGERS: Oh, no. I really must go.

JUD: If Harry were here he'd give us a dance. Or happen sing us a song.

MISS ROGERS: Stop talking about him, Mr. Slater. It's morbid to go on like this. You must think of the living, not the dead.

JUD: (Empties glass, pours more whiskey)
It's the dead I care about, lass.

MISS ROGERS: Don't drink any more, Mr. Slater.

JUD: Aren't you lonely, lass?

MISS ROGERS: Lonely? No. I'm with people all day long.

JUD: So am I. (Empties glass, pours more whiskey) If you can call that lot people.

MISS ROGERS: Don't drink any more.

JUD: I'm that lonely. Sometimes I think my head'll burst. I think that last thing I'll see is what bit of brains I've got flying all over this shed.

MISS ROGERS: You must stop coming in here. You must stop sitting in here all alone.

JUD: Mun I, lass? (Drinks) Where will I sit then? In that kitchen with her? In that house I was born in? That house is full of bogeys. There's one laughing at me from every corner. (Empties glass, pours more whiskey) I'm trapped. I've been trapped all these years, like a rabbit in yon fields. I've heard of rabbits biting their paws off so they can get away to die somewhere else. (Bangs his head with his fist) I'm trapped up here. What can I do? Bite me bloody head off?

MISS ROGERS: Don't talk like this, Mr. Slater.

JUD: We were only fourteen when they nailed us. They hauled us before the magistrates and put us away.

MISS ROGERS: I don't understand. Don't drink any more. What had you done?

JUD: Then when we were sixteen they let us out on condition we got married. (Empties glass) They might as well have kept us in.

MISS ROGERS: (Puts the top on the whiskey bottle, moves it away from him)
This isn't beer, Mr. Slater. You're not used to it.

JUD: We only had the one child, you know. Just the one. They put the fear of Christ in us. I'll have that bottle, lass.

MISS ROGERS: (Picks up the bottle) You've had enough to drink.

JUD: (Rises and stands over her. MISS ROGERS holds the bottle away from him)
I'm the best judge of that. Hand me the bottle then.
(Makes a sudden move and takes the bottle from her)
There's enough folk order me about. Don't you start, lass.

JUD: (CONT'D)
(Tries to pour whiskey into his glass, but the top is on. He tries to take the top off, but is unable to. He smashes the top off against the edge of the generator. MISS ROGERS gets hurriedly to her feet, JUD pours whiskey into his glass)
Xmas, eh? Merry bloody Xmas then.

MISS ROGERS: I'm going now. I have to pack. I'll get Mrs. Slater to put you to bed.

JUD:
(Drinks, puts glass on housing of generator)
You'll do no such thing. Her's _never_ been in here.
(Goes towards her, drunk now and desperate for a comforting word)
I'm tormented. Do you understand, lass? I've gone grey waiting for Harry to come through that door. Would they have let him wear his clogs, do you think?

MISS ROGERS: I must go now.

JUD: I meant to tell them. Christ knows I meant to. I know he didn't do it.

MISS ROGERS: You think he didn't do it. You can't _know._

JUD: I know, all right. If I'd told them what I know Harry would still be dancing through the fields.

MISS ROGERS: Why _didn't_ you tell them then?
(JUD goes to her. He lifts his hand to her head as though to stroke her hair, then collapses into a chair. MISS ROGERS puts her hand below his chin and lifts his head. JUD gazes unblinkingly at her)
Why didn't you tell them?

JUD:
(Almost without inflection)
They'd have hung me then, you see.

MISS ROGERS:
(Takes her hand away) You!

JUD: Her created so. I only wanted to hush her. I carried her to the cut and dropped her in. She floated. I stood there waiting for her to sink, but her were still floating when I ran away with her screams dinning in my ears... Dadda... Dadda... Her kept screaming on and on... Dadda... Till I hushed her.

MISS ROGERS: Dadda?

JUD: Ay, lass. Our Nellie still called me dadda. I reckon she were fond of me.

JUD: (CONT'D)

(SARAH enters upstage right, goes to lectern, takes book and goes down to the table. She sits and opens the book.

JUD slumps to his knees. His head goes close to the floor to give the dead a better chance to hear. MISS ROGERS moves away, then stands watching him)

Forgive me... Forgive me, our Nellie... Forgive me, Harry lad. (Lifts his head) Do you think they will, lass?

(Gets to his feet, approaches her, arms extended as though to enfold her)

Do you think they will?

(MISS ROGERS runs away and up, collapses sobbing on the single bed. SARAH raises her head from the book, listening)

I've done it now, Floss. I'm feared I've done it now.

(Stands motionless for a moment, then goes slowly across to door down right, through the door and up to SARAH)

SARAH: What have you been doing out there all this time? You've been out there for hours.

JUD: Where's yon lass?

SARAH: (Closes book) Who do you love, our Jud? Say who you love.

JUD: There's not time for that now, Sarah. Did yon lass come in?

SARAH: I heard her go to her room not a minute ago. Her tea's still on the hob. Fat lot I care whether she eats it or not.

JUD: Thank Christ for that... I've done it now, Sarah. Christ knows I've done it now.

SARAH: Done what? (Rises) Has Miss Gutsy been in that shed again?

JUD: Ay.

SARAH: She gave me her solemn word.

(Goes closer to JUD, book still in her arms)

Have you been drinking?

JUD: Ay. I had an Xmas drink. It's nearly Xmas time out there, you know.

SARAH: She gave me her solemn word she wouldn't go in that shed again. Did you try to interfere with her?

JUD: We had a drink, I tell you. An Xmas drink.

SARAH: Where's my Xmas drink then?

JUD: I wish I'd ne'er seen that bloody bottle. I told her, Sarah.

SARAH: (The book crashes to floor)
Told her! You told her!

JUD: Ay.

SARAH: You drunken fool, Jud.

JUD: Her'll happen think it were only the drink talking.

SARAH: Not her. Her'll be on her bike and at that police station if we don't stop her.

JUD: I doubt she'll go to the police.

SARAH: She'll go to the police.

JUD: If she does she does. We can't stop her.

SARAH: We can stop her, Jud. (Moves nearer to him) We can stop her.
(JUD puts a hand to his teeth, moving backwards away from her as he does so. SARAH goes slowly up to the single bed. MISS ROGERS raises her head from the pillow)
I hear you've been in that shed again.
(MISS ROGERS nods her head)
Once too often this time, was it?
(MISS ROGERS again nods her head)
You gave me your solemn word. You're all like that, aren't you? With your fancy ways and your books and your soft voices. All you well off folk are like that. You give your word as easy as you give a good morning to the milkman. And you think no more of it, either. We're not like that. You should have stayed with your own sort.

MISS ROGERS: (Sits upright) How can you live with him? Your own daughter! You cook his meals and clean his house and he killed your daughter. You share his bed. His bed.

SARAH: It was his child too. I'm married to him. I gave my solemn word I'd stick to him and I'll keep my word. I'll cook his meals and clean his house and share his bed till I see him under. He's my man. He's the only man I've ever known and I'll stick to him.

MISS ROGERS: How can you stand it? How can you wake up each day and look at him?

SARAH: It's my life and I live it. I have a duty and I do it.

MISS ROGERS: (Rises from bed) I'm leaving now, Mrs. Slater. I'll send someone for my things in the morning. Please ask your husband to get my bicycle out of the shed.

SARAH: (Doesn't move, doesn't turn her head. Calls) Jud.

JUD: (Softly, almost to himself) What is it then?

SARAH: Come in here.
(JUD goes slowly up to them. SARAH and MISS ROGERS stand unmoving, facing each other. As JUD joins them:)
She wants her bike.

JUD: I'll get it then.

SARAH: You'll do no such thing. She's not going anywhere just yet.

MISS ROGERS: I am leaving immediately. Get my bicycle, Mr. Slater. (To SARAH) I don't intend to tell anyone, if that's what you're afraid of.

JUD: I were only codding, lass, in the shed just now. You didn't believe me, did you?

MISS ROGERS: Yes. I believed you. Your own daughter. You let them hang your friend. The only friend you've ever had.

JUD: Nay, you're wrong. There's Flossie. I have got Flossie.

MISS ROGERS: Flossie.

SARAH: Shut up, Jud

JUD: She won't tell anybody, Sarah. She said she won't. You won't go to the police, will you, lass? You'll only look like a fool when I tell them I were codding.

MISS ROGERS: I know you were telling the truth, but I won't go to the police. What good would that do?

JUD: That's right. It would only cause more trouble.

MISS ROGERS: Will you get my bicycle?

JUD: (Turns) Ay.

SARAH: You'll stay where you are. I'll tell you when to get that bike.

JUD: (Turns back) Let her go, Sarah. Let her go.

SARAH: (Ignores him) I don't doubt you'll give us your word that you won't let on to the police. Or anybody else, for that matter.

MISS ROGERS: Of course I will.

SARAH: Your solemn word?

MISS ROGERS: Of course. Now may I go?

SARAH: As I recall it you gave your word to me once before. It didn't take you long to break it. How long will you keep it this time?

MISS ROGERS: I'll keep my word, Mrs. Slater. I'll never break it. Don't you see it's different this time?

SARAH: Is it? What way is it different then?

MISS ROGERS: This is important. I would never break my word on something important.

SARAH: Wouldn't you? Your solemn word is your solemn word. If you break it once you'll break it again. I don't trust you. It were folk like you who put us away. It were folk like you who turned us into what we are. This is a sad house, but it weren't always sad. There were laughter here at one time. I can still hear it now and again when I wake up early on a windy morning. The wind wakes it in its hiding places. It were folk like you who killed the laughter here.

MISS ROGERS: Like me! I wasn't even born then.

JUD: (Hopelessly) Let her go. Let her go now, Sarah.

SARAH: Our Nellie brought it back for a while, but the damage had been done. Jud here turned her into a cold, wet thing, but who turned him into a father who could do that to his own child? (Her voice is raised now) You lot did it. You lot with your fancy ways and your clean hands. You treated us like dirty, twisted things and you turned us into dirty, twisted things.

MISS ROGERS: I'm going now. Please let me pass.

SARAH: (Pushes her back. MISS ROGERS loses balance and falls back on to the bed)
You'll go when I say you can go and not before. You've changed your minds on things like that now, but only because it suits you. You can change your minds about every mortal thing in creation and it won't help us. Do you hear me? It won't help me and Jud.

SARAH: (CONT'D) — (Advances on MISS ROGERS, who cowers on the bed)
You say you won't tell. I know you won't tell. I'll make sure you don't tell.

MISS ROGERS: (Suddenly upright on the bed, tries to move away)
Mr. Slater! What is your wife doing, Mr. Slater? What is she --
(SARAH is on her. MISS ROGERS threshes wildly on the bed, but she is no match for the hard strength of SARAH, who soon has her flat on her back, with a knee on each shoulder. MISS ROGERS' legs kick up and down, touching nothing but the air)

JUD: (Almost to himself) Let her go, Sarah. I'm for letting her go.
(MISS ROGERS begins to scream. Moan-like at first, then full bodied and terrible. JUD stands as though caught in a snare. SARAH reaches for the pillow, raises it, then lowers it. The screams are cut off. The legs kick frantically, then more slowly. One leg gives a last convulsive kick, then they are still. All is quiet.

JUD moves as though breaking away from something)
Her's done for.
(Raises a hand as though to touch SARAH's shoulder. The hand moves away and falls to his side)
You can take the pillow off.

SARAH: (Removes pillow) Ay. Her'll keep her word now.
(Rises, straightens her dress) Her were a loud un.

JUD: Ay. I shouldn't be surprised if they heard her in Loston.

SARAH: They'll take no notice if they did. There's screams on the telly night after night. A few extra won't bother them.

JUD: Do you mind telling me what we're going to do now?

SARAH: We'll wait a while till we're sure there'll be nobody about. Then we'll put her on her bike and take her a good two or three mile away from here and push her in the cut, bike and all. They'll think she lost her way and rode into it in the dark.

JUD: They'll cut her up. They'll know she didn't drown. They'll know there's been some dirty work.

SARAH: Let 'em. We'll tell them we thought she'd gone to her new place tonight. There's nothing to show she came back here.

JUD: They're not that daft. They'll put two and two together.

SARAH: They made two and two twenty-two last time and they'll make it twenty-two again.

JUD: Her were a bonny lass. That skin. (Puts hand on her hair) Her hair's that soft. (His hand moves to her face) Her's as warm as toast.

SARAH: Hands off, Jud.

JUD: I'm only touching. Just touching.

SARAH: I said hands off.

JUD: (Takes hand away) It's not right. Christ, what a bloody shame.

SARAH: You don't still expect things to be right, do you? They haven't been right for us for a long time. Why should they be right for her? She had everything handed to her on a plate, and at that I'll bet somebody had to show her where her mouth was. Miss Rogers. Miss Pamela Rogers. Well, she's not Miss Rogers now. She's a carcass that'll soon start to smell.

JUD: You're a hard woman, Sarah.

SARAH: What made me hard then? I were soft as putty once. I were softer than she's ever been.

JUD: Are you not sorry for her then?

SARAH: Why should I be sorry? She was just six pounds a week to me. And a mouth that did its best to eat up all the profit. She came here lording it over us with her fancy talk. Why should I be sorry for her?

JUD: She had so much to look forward to.

SARAH: So did I at one time. If you want to feel sorry for somebody feel sorry for me... Is there any of that whiskey left?

JUD: Ay.

SARAH: (Moves away) Bring it into the parlour then. (SARAH moves towards table. Picks scrapbook up, places it on the table as she sits. JUD goes down to the generator, picks up bottle and glasses and goes up and across to the table)

SARAH: You've been hiding things from me. Money in your pocket and you didn't say. What a waste spending it on whiskey.

JUD: (Sits, pours into the glasses, passes one to SARAH) There should be summat special for Xmas.

SARAH: It's Xmas for them. They'll all go back to work broke dreaming of another spree at Easter. (Drinks) It's not Xmas for us. We'll have our Xmas later when they don't know where their next meal's coming from. It's in the Midland. Safe. I'll see you're all right, Jud. There'll always be a home for you here.

JUD: (Drinks, slams glass down) What if I don't want it then?

SARAH: (Complacently) This is your home, Jud.

JUD: You've lost sight of something important, Sarah. It wasn't me who snuffed yon lass's candle out. It were you. You haven't got the hold over me now that you had a few minutes ago.

SARAH: Haven't I? You don't think I've hung on to you all these years to lose you now, do you?

JUD: I've got something on you now. We're either both trapped or both free. (Rises) You can keep this house. You can keep all that's in it. You can keep that bloody money in the bank, but you can't keep me. Come Sunday and I'm off.

SARAH: The police would be after you then, wouldn't they?

JUD: What for? There's no law against a man leaving his wife so long as he doesn't leave her homeless.

SARAH: It's yon lass they'll be after you for, Jud.

JUD: Yon lass? You did for her, not me.

SARAH: Not me, Jud. (Rises) You did. I heard her screaming and rushed in and there you were with the pillow over her face, trying to interfere with her. I'll tell them you didn't mean to kill her, by the looks of it. You didn't mean to kill our Nellie either, did you?

JUD: (Moves away) Her created so.

SARAH: I've a double hold on you now. Here you are and here you'll stay.

JUD: (Stands still, lost eyes avoiding hers) I mun get away.

SARAH: You'll get away one day. There's room for two more in that grave. First you and then me. I'll see you're put away nicely and leave instructions and enough money for me to go on top. We'll all be comfy then. All together again. In the meantime you'll carry on as usual. You'll go to work and come home to your good teas. You'll scrub my back every Saturday night. You'll sleep with me in that bed. You'll meet me at yon graveyard every Sunday. And when I say pray, our Jud, you'll pray.

JUD: (Breaks away) Nay, I'll not.
(Goes across and down towards generator, turns and shouts)
I'll bloody not. (Gets his bicycle) I'm off now. (His hand goes to generator housing) Good-bye, Floss. (Shouts) Do you hear me? I'm off now.
(JUD wheels his bicycle left. SARAH stands watching him. As he nears extremity of setting she opens the scrapbook on the table. The portrait of "Our Nellie" becomes visible)

SARAH: Jud!

JUD: (Stops, does not turn) What is it then?

SARAH: Come here.
(JUD turns, goes slowly back to generator, stands near it)
Jud!

JUD: (Leans bicycle against generator)
She'll scream her head off one day, Floss.

SARAH: What's keeping you, our Jud?

JUD: All right then.
(Goes slowly up and across to SARAH)
What is it then?

SARAH: (Holds open book in both hands in front of her)
I bore this child with every hand and tongue against me. I bore this child in a place of green walls and uniforms. I were but fourteen, but I swore I'd keep my child. I were but fourteen and they had no mercy. It weren't for the want of asking. I went down on my knees in this very room. "Don't let them take me away, my mam. Don't let them take me away." But they came with their uniforms and their motor cars.
(JUD, his blank eyes fixed on the book, is motionless near her. SARAH cradles book in her arms)
I've ne'er asked for mercy since.

SARAH: (CONT'D) (Gently rocks book)
Hush then. Not even when they brought her home that night all wet and cold. They came with their uniforms and their motor cars then too. They stood there waiting for me to break down, but I wouldn't give them that satisfaction. "Put her on the kitchen table," I said. "I'll wash her and put her a clean nightie on." "She'll have to go to the mortuary," they said. "She'll be washed there." "I'll wash her," I said. "I washed her when she came into this hell hole and I'll wash her now." Her were blue and that cold. It were all I could do to get the nightie on her. (Rocks book in cradled arms) Then they took her away and I ne're saw her again.

JUD: I'll have the book now, Sarah.

SARAH: I'm not asking for mercy now. I'm telling you, our Jud. You'll stay.

JUD: Ay. Give me the book then.
(JUD takes the book from her. He closes it, goes up to lectern, puts book on it. The portrait of "Our Nellie" fades and disappears. JUD turns back to SARAH)

SARAH: We'll have a lie down for an hour or so, then we'll get shut of Miss Gutsy.

JUD: Ay.
(SARAH crosses to double bed. JUD watches her, then slowly follows her. SARAH takes shoes off and lies down fully dressed. JUD sits on chair to right of bed. He takes his boots off)
There'll be no more lodgers.
(A moment's silence)
Do you hear me, Sarah? I say there'll be no more lodgers.

SARAH: It's a shame to waste a nice room like that. There's some would be glad of it.

JUD: Them Pakis. Twenty to a room.

SARAH: All right, Jud. There'll be just the two of us from now on.

JUD: (Lies fully dressed on the bed) Ay.
(Silence. Then:)

SARAH: Who do you love then?
(They lie with heads high on the pillows gazing straight ahead)
Say who you love.

SARAH: (CONT'D) Say who you. love.

(Each raises the nearer hand. The two hands move slowly towards each other)

<u>Say who you love.</u>

JUD: You, Sarah. Only you.

(As the two pairs of eyes gaze unblinkingly straight ahead the two hands find and hold each other)

THE END